Table of Contents

Prophetic Art

A Practical Guide to Creating with
the Holy Spirit

by Matt Tommey

Prophetic Art
A Practical Guide to Creating with the Holy Spirit

Introduction

The opportunity to co-create with the Creator of All is simply mind blowing. And yet, that is His invitation; to cooperate with Him through the power of the Holy Spirit; to reveal, reflect and release His image, nature and presence into the world through our creative expression. All He asks from us is our yes! He doesn't ask for perfection. Or even for us to be highly qualified. He asks for our yes — because He knows if we will yield to the Spirit in our process — He will bring the results He desires.

Relationship

Everything in the Kingdom is birthed through intimate relationship with God through the Holy Spirit. In fact, Jesus taught how vital our relationship with Him is to our growth and fruit production in life when He said:

"Remain in me, as I also remain in you. No branch can bear fruit by itself; it must remain in the vine. Neither can you bear fruit unless you remain in me. I am the vine; you are the branches. If you remain in me and I in you, you will bear much fruit; apart from me you can do nothing." John 15:4-5 NIV

As you cultivate a vital, life-giving relationship with Jesus, the Holy Spirit will speak to you, lead and guide you into all truth (John 16:13).

Creativity After the Fall

After the fall of man, Adam's sin built a wall and brought a curse. Adam went from thriving by God's grace to striving in his own strength through painful toil and the sweat of his brow (Genesis 3:17-19). Unfortunately, he passed that same curse and pattern on to his sons and they passed it on to theirs, on and on to us.

Until Jesus' finished work on the cross redeemed us from the curse and restored the full inheritance of the Kingdom to us. As believer's, we no longer have to strive on our own. If you do, it's completely your choice and the result of an unrenewed mind.

As new covenant believers, we can live lives empowered by the Holy Spirit with access to every Kingdom resource in the storehouse of heaven (Deuteronomy 28:12). Every resource, relationship, opportunity and idea are at our disposal. All we'll ever need is already provided for us in abundance (2 Peter 1:3-4).

Your gift of creativity is God's investment in you. How you operate that powerful engine is up to you. You can choose to walk as a son - receiving everything you need by faith that God has provided by grace - or as an orphan - begging and striving because you believe it's all up to you. Creative expression absent the power and presence of God is often beautiful but rarely transformative.

Prophetic Art offers Transformation

When your artistic creations are Spirit-birthed – a skillfully produced incarnation – they become a conduit for transformation. Not because of us or our talent but because our art carries the Light and Life

– the very nature – of God. Just like God communes with His people through the sacrament of communion when the simple bread and wine become a means of grace, our prophetic art has the capacity throughout time to speak and continue speaking to everyone who encounters it. Like the stone cairns that you see throughout the Celtic landscape of Scotland. These stacked stone monuments act as reminders that in the middle of what seems like nowhere, there is a trail marking our way. Our artwork and creative expression are opportunities to set up spiritual intersections for generations to come. Songs that will be sung long after we are gone, buildings that will stand for centuries, declaring God's Glory, and even tangible works of art that we create; all acting as intersection points where God shows up and connects with His children.

A Transformative Intersection

My friend, Jörn Lange has been a missionary and artist in Cyprus for many years, seeing the power and presence of God move through His artwork. He shared one such story with me:

"*We organize an art outreach every year at the biggest fair here in Cyprus around the time of Pentecost. The entire seafront becomes a festival where we offer prophetic art to the passers-by, pray for the inspiration of the Holy Spirit, and sketch or paint spontaneously what He shows us. Artists work in two-hour shifts every day from 11:00 a.m. to 11:00 for eight to ten days during the fair.*

In 2017, a young local came into our tent with his girlfriend and another acquaintance. My then 15-year-old son was volunteering and the three of them sat down. I talked with Manos while my son prayed and painted. When he was done, his painting was divided in two. On one side it was dark and a whirlwind was in the middle with a bright light on the other side. Manos did not speak any English but his acquaintance offered to interpret for us.

Our approach is to ask questions about the painting and to answer questions from the recipients. We do not give unsolicited advice or messages. We asked Manos what he saw in the painting. Manos immediately looked at the dark side of the painting and explained that this showed what he was involved in. My son jumped a little when he realized what these things were. Manos continued by saying that he wanted to get out of those things, but every time he tried, there would be something like a storm drawing him back in. He then asked how to get to the light on the other side of the painting. At this moment, my son asked him to give him the painting back. He had seen a red bridge appear over the whirlwind. Manos asked what this bridge was. We explained, "We believe Jesus is the bridge, the way to help you cross over the storm into the light. The red is a symbol for Christ's blood". Manos asked why there needed to be blood and a deeper conversation ensued. We explained the gospel three times.

He continued to ask questions. Manos asked us how he could start a relationship with Jesus. and we explained what it meant to ask for forgiveness of his sins (the dark side of the painting) and to decide to follow Jesus (the light side). Manos then prayed in Greek to receive Christ. He beamed, the change in him showing all over his face. He asked us what he should do if the dark side came again to grab him. I explained how the Gospel of John tells us God is light and Jesus is the light of the world. I then suggested he do two things when the darkness came again: read the Gospel of John, and to loudly proclaim that Jesus is the light. He took a New Testament in modern Greek, thanked us, and left."

Are you ready to find out more about prophetic art and creating with the Holy Spirit? Then you're in the right place! This comprehensive guide to prophetic creativity and the inspiring personal stories of varied artists and writers included here will help you get started creating with the Holy Spirit in a deeper, more meaningful way. That is the point of this book. To give you the language, framework and vision for entering into the creative process with the Holy Spirit so that the creative expression of your life becomes transformational for you and those who come in contact with your work.

Matt Tommey

The Spiritual Function of Art

Art, like any other created means, is a vehicle for the presence of God to move in and through. Art functions almost as a stealth language by which God can commune with us as Kingdom artists, as well as speak to the viewer in beautiful ways that bypass the cognitive, left-brain processing of information. Art speaks directly to the emotion, beauty and desire portions of our brain. It goes deep and can be used to affect significant change.

Artist Kate Green describes her creative process, saying *"Over the years God's taught me to hear His voice and to share what He's saying through colors, which I've discovered have a language that can speak to anyone whatever their age or faith. So I'll have a conversation with God where a color jumps out at me in some sort of setting and He'll unpack new ways to communicate something of his kingdom to people through that color.*

When I'm doing a painting, especially in a public setting, I talk with God before I paint and he gives me an idea of a theme, then we chat about the colors and composition. I don't know what it will look like in detail but I always start with a title and a bible passage that it links to, and some sort of color plan. Then while I'm painting, I try to respond to what the Holy Spirit is wanting to do in that setting, it can often involve some prophetic action e.g. pouring paint down the canvas when I feel God is pouring himself over us, or creating tears and then wiping them with a sense of God wanting to bring comfort.

And then I love is taking these pictures, created in a place of worship and encounter with God, into secular spaces and share them with people who don't know him. They're fascinated by the freedom and cheerfulness, the energy & joy of my work (it draws them in). They want to know more and to take it home with them!"

God can and will use your prophetic art to:

- Reveal God's Beauty & Nature
- Demonstrate a Kingdom Truth in a Fresh and Unusual Way
- Bring Healing Physically, Emotionally, Spiritually or Mentally.
- Awaken Wonder and Revelation by the Spirit
- Quicken Conviction of the Holy Spirit
- Offer Salvation to Someone Who Doesn't Yet Know the Lord
- Confirm the Ongoing Work of the Spirit in Someone's Life

Artist Aeron Brown shares about how God first awakened the gift of prophetic creativity in his life:

"It was my first live painting back in 2005, I was asked to paint a word from God for the congregation of my church. I was terrified. I asked God for an image... any image. I saw a hand holding a heart with an unlocked treasure chest within it. I was angry because it didn't seem cool or an image I wanted to paint, but it was the only image I had so I begrudgingly painted that image. Afterwards I felt like a complete dork. I was packing up my supplies when a woman in tears came up

to me. She told me that she hadn't been in church for a long time and was angry at God after she had gone through some difficult things in church. She felt like her heart had been locked towards God even though she missed experiencing Him. That night when she saw me about to paint, she prayed and asked God to paint her heart being unlocked to prove to her that God was real and that he would heal her heart. That was the very image God gave me. I was so amazed. After seeing how my art impacted that woman, I decided I would paint prophetic paintings for the rest of my life in the hope others might experience the same thing. I'm still creating prophetic images today with hundreds of stories to tell."

God also uses the creative process to move in the life of the artist. Years of research prove how creative outlets provide a cathartic way for people to process and move through trauma, addiction, abuse and other life-dominating issues. As we create, God heals, convicts, draws and leads us. Consider the way David processed life through his music and poetry. Throughout the Psalms, we see him move from complaining to rejoicing in God. This practice brought peace to his soul and helped him work out his issues with God.

Author, Jody Thomae describes the transformative experience of creating in this way;

"As an author, I paint pictures with words. Before I begin to write, I have spent a great deal of time in study, preparation and meditating on the scripture passages I might use in my writing. Usually in this study process there'll be something that rises to the surface--an "aha" moment, an epiphany. So, when I sit down to write, I often have an idea of what I'm going to say. However, when I begin typing--and this has happened over and over to me--I get a sense of the Holy Spirit speaking directly to me, to my own heart, deep within my spirit. I often have to stop and take it in. In fact, you can often find me crying at my writing desk... touched deeply by what God is saying in the moment. I sense that God wants me to hear first what I'm writing and THEN share it with others."

I've experienced the same thing in my own life. Whether it be in the planning of a worship set, writing a song or a book, creating a piece of art or even gardening at my home; God is always speaking. As I tune my ears to His voice, my creative process becomes a means of grace where I am changed again into His image.

What is Prophetic Art?

Simply put, prophetic art is creating art with God for the purpose of transforming those that see it and create it. It's a beautiful dance where we as artists cooperate with the Holy Spirit. As we pursue the art God has put on our heart, He inspires us, equips us, and brings fulfillment to our unique design while releasing His transformative nature.

Remember, everything in the Kingdom is birthed through intimate relationship with God through the Holy Spirit. Without it, we easily end up striving in our own strength rather than thriving in God's grace.

Prophetic Art Releases God's Beauty

Through the prophetic creative process, we release the beauty of God for all to see. We release Heaven's perspective into a dark and broken world, offering life, love and hope to all who encounter our work.

As our artistic skills increase and our capacity to flow with God is enlarged, our ability to hear the voice of the Holy Spirit is sharpened. Our art then becomes much more than just the sum of materials, tools and techniques. It becomes both redemptive and transformative, a means of grace to everyone who encounters it.

Creating with the Holy Spirit is more about the process than the product, more about the intention than the outcome. It's about cultivating ears to hear, eyes to see, and senses to feel what God is saying and doing within your world. Then, responding through your chosen creative process. That's prophetic art.

Come and Dine

One of the best metaphors I love to use to illustrate the varied ways art releases God's Light and Life is that of a table. Our artwork becomes, as in Psalm 23, a table prepared to nourish those who come and sit before the King. And in His presence, everything that seeks to kill, suppress and confuse them is demolished.

Oh to think of it! The very expression of your heart and hands can be used to demonstrate the transforming love of God. You see my friend, prophetic art and beauty are not merely ornamental, they touch the very nature of the creator God.

Prophetic art should never be forced into typical Christian metaphor or preconceived notions of what it should or shouldn't look like. The exciting thing about art is the mystery of its creation and interpretation. The ways God can use prophetic art are endless.

Over the years God has shown up in incredible ways through my artwork. From ushering in the presence of God through a song I wrote, to lives being changed through the words I've written; God is faithful to use the work of our hands for His glory!

Once, when I was doing a "meet and greet" demonstration at a local gallery, a man was drawn to particular piece of woven sculpture I created. Transfixed, he exclaimed; "It's like the hands of God are reaching out and He is saying I have everything under control!" I was astonished and yet not surprised. That's how God works! He uses the foolish and unseemly things to speak to those who are listening.

Why not YOU? Why not YOUR art?

As an artist in the Kingdom, and more importantly a child of God, it is vital that you realize you were created for greatness! The spirit of excellence, power and healing that resides in His DNA resides in you. The creativity that dreamed and formed everything you know as life today is your inheritance in Christ. Through your salvation in Him, you now have a new DNA that has been downloaded into the core of who you are.

God does not play favorites. The more you enlarge your capacity for His presence by becoming excellent at what you do, the more the Father will entrust to you. That's how you grow in the Kingdom.

Prophetic creativity is God's idea and the Lord invites every artist to create with Him. Only three things are required:

- Inviting Holy Spirit to Join You in the Studio
- Listening to His Voice as You're Making Art
- Responding in Faith through Your Creative Process

The Historical and Biblical Impact of Prophetic Art

The History of Prophetic Art

There is a rich heritage of artists throughout history who connected their work with the divine inspiration of God.

The famous composer Johann Sebastian Bach believed: *"The aim and final end of all music should be none other than the glory of God and the refreshment of the soul."*

Rembrandt concluded; "*A painting is complete when it has the shadows of God*" and "*Painting is the grandchild of nature. It is related to God.*"

French author, Andre Gide said; "*Art is a collaboration between God and artist, and the less the artist does, the better.*"

From the earliest years of Christianity (and prior to Jesus in the Jewish tradition), artists and artisans worked in tandem with religious leaders to create works of art and environments where people could experience the beauty and majesty of God. Much of this found it's home in houses of worship where sculptures like Michelangelo's Pieta and others are so majestically displayed. Michelangelo in particular had a very strong spiritual connection with his work, stating: "*Art is the gift of God and must be used to His glory. That in art is highest which aims at this.*"

Unfortunately, when the protestant reformation came on the scene, much of this creative culture was severely diminished or even lost. For many, beautiful music and historic hymns of the church became empty performance. Majestic architecture originally built for the glory of God now a relic of times gone by. Worship became sterile and disconnected itself from the very nature of our beautiful God. Fortunately, there have always been those who pressed in for more! Even now, attitudes in the church toward creativity and beauty are shifting back toward embracing the fullness of God.

It was late 90's /early 2000's when I saw artist Janice VanCronkhite in Atlanta, Georgia painting on stage during worship. I was amazed and stunned by the beauty of her prophetic painting and the expressive intuition she flowed with as she painted. That's the first time I can remember hearing the term "prophetic art". While these artistic expressions are becoming more common in the life of the church, they used to be seen primarily in Charismatic / Non-denominational churches. Now it's not uncommon to find visual artists, dancers, media teams, sculptors and the like as integral parts of the church's worship experience around the world within every stream of the Body of Christ.

Worship art has become its own "genre" of art. Artist's often work with the worship team to create spontaneous works of prophetic art to enhance the worship experience for the congregation. It's another way to visually display what God is saying to His people. How beautiful!

The Biblical Basis for Prophetic Art

You might be wondering yourself if there is scriptural evidence of this idea of creating with God. Yes, I can emphatically tell you it does. All throughout the Bible we see instances of God calling people to create objects, demonstrations and environments that He could use in the context of revealing His Glory, Beauty, and Nature-- bringing the Kingdom to the earth.

Consider these Biblical examples:

- Noah created an ark that rescued humanity and the animals in order to fulfill God's redemptive and restorative plan.
- Bezalel led a team that created the Tabernacle of Moses which became God's dwelling place among His people.
- Moses, led by the spirit, threw down a wooden staff that supernaturally became a serpent in front of the Pharaoh.

- David created his Tabernacle with 24/7 worship for 30+ years that became the place where God's presence would abide with his people.
- Solomon created the Temple including all the symbolic furniture and items inside, which served as the center of worship for the people of God.
- Psalm 19 says the Heavens declare the glory of God and the earth shows forth His handiwork.
- Balaam's donkey literally spoke to him while enabled by the Spirit of God.
- Jeremiah used the analogy of the potter and the clay to demonstrate God's forming and guiding hands in the lives of the Israelites.
- Hosea married a prostitute to show the reality of God's unchanging love in tangible form.
- Jesus spit into the dirt, made a mud ball, and used it as a means to restore a man's sight.
- Paul, in Ephesians, refers to humanity as the "poema" of God; a masterpiece or poem.

Bezalel! What a Guy!

The first picture in the Bible of an artist like this is a guy named Bezalel. Plucked out of seeming obscurity, he was elevated to a place of influence designed specifically by God for him.

I love digging deep to find the meanings of each word in the Bible. As you read the scripture verses below with what I learned in parentheses, try to imagine the kind of person and artist Bezalel was.

"See, I have called" (to publicly proclaim) "Bezalel" (in the shadow or protection of God), son of "Uri" (the fiery one, light, prophetic revelation), the son of "Hur" (white or pure), of the tribe of "Judah" (praise)" and I have "filled" (overflowing) him with the "Spirit" (breath or wind) of God, with wisdom, with "understanding" (skillful discernment), with "knowledge" (an intimate knowing) and in all manner of "craftsmanship" (occupation or work, as an ambassador, angel or messenger).

I took the descriptive words above and paraphrased them. I hope this gives you a clearer picture of *your* calling:

Our identity as artists is that of sons and daughters, publicly affirmed and sent by the Father to walk as fiery torches of prophetic revelation in the earth while creating from a place of purity and praise in the shadow and protection of God's presence. In that place, we have been given an overflowing impartation of the living breath of God and brought into His intimate presence to be sent as divinely equipped prophetic messengers, carrying His authority.

Just like Bezalel, you have been specifically designed and called by God to be an artist, an image-bearer, a glory-releaser in the earth. You're designed to co-labor with the Father in releasing His Kingdom out of a place of intimacy and purity with Him. When perfectionism and the voice of your inner critic raises its ugly sound-- and it will-- resist! Stand upon God's promises! Press into His truth! As you meditate on your calling and reflect in your journal what this means for you, let gratitude arise for all God has created you to be.

The God-Inspired Artist

God is creative and we are created in His image. Therefore, we are creative. And if God is the source of all creativity, then our search for ultimate creativity must be rooted and grounded in Him. Our search for creativity begins with God. It is really our search for the fullness of God in and throughout our life.

From the very beginning of time, art was God's idea. It is by Him and through Him and for Him. Yet as His children, it is also by us, through us and for us (and others). What a collaboration!

When we place our trust in Jesus and receive Him as Lord, we become what the Bible calls "new creations" through the power of the Holy Spirit. The fullness of that identity is activated in our life through faith. We don't have to do anything but receive the gift from the Father. He's done all the work. For each of us, our life as a new creation is different, based on how He has wired us.

The same is true when we tap into the creativity of Heaven to create new physical creations (2 Corinthians 5:17). The creative DNA of Heaven living inside of us is always active, always on, always ready for us to access (John 5:16ff). When we function in the realm of Christ – agreeing with what God says is true – the flow of Heaven's creativity is activated. Inspired by the movement of the Holy Spirit in, around and through us; we create.

God inspires artists to create prophetic art in a variety of ways because each artist is unique. What inspires me may not inspire you, and vice versa. To think that all artists are inspired in the same way is to limit how God speaks to us. Even though many artists struggle to believe God is speaking to them, rest assured, God is always speaking. The question is: are we listening as intuitively as we can in order to hear Him in the nuances of our lives?

Our Creative Well

The idea of an inner source of creativity is one that most artists identify with on a visceral level, although not always able to articulate. Julia Cameron, in her incredible book *The Artist's Way*, gives voice to this concept. She describes this source as an inner reservoir or well that must be refilled in order to release a fresh flow of inspiration when you need it. This well holds the inspiration we collect, cultivate, and curate throughout our lives. I love that because many artists assume that their creative well is going to refill itself. It won't. We must be as intentional about cultivating inspiration as we are about creating the expression of it. Make it a daily practice to note the things that inspire you and intentionally focus on them. This intentional and focused practice will release a fresh flow of Spirit-led creativity when you do get in the studio.

As I have sought to understand this beautiful concept, The Holy Spirit revealed a number of important ideas regarding how inspiration must be cultivated and stewarded in our life. Central to my understanding is that the Holy Spirit moves over all the inspiration we sow into our heart and mind, allowing us to co-labor with Him in the creative process. As we are continually filled with His Spirit (Ephesians 5:18) both personally and artistically we create from a place of overflow.

Like the woman at the well, we often approach our creativity outside of a life-giving relationship with Jesus. Don't get me wrong. It's not always out of impure motives. Sometimes you don't know what you don't know. And so, we show up doing the best we can with what know at the time, even though we might feel defeated, marginalized, or unworthy. We look for the flowing water of inspiration but find it fleeting. Our cisterns are broken, and our wells have run dry. Some often describe this as experiencing "creative block".

That doesn't have to be your normal! Jesus offers us a flowing river of living water. He alone is the well that never runs dry. He is the source of all creativity and the one who desires to release His creative flow in and through our life. We cooperate with this process by intentionally entering his presence, being continually filled with the Holy Spirit and creating with Him. As we create with Him, look for inspiration, listen for His voice and cultivate a sense of wonder in our life, we will find a never-ending river of creative inspiration flowing through our life.

Prophetic Percolation

Inspiration is constantly available for artists, both internally and externally. I think of those creative ideas like coffee beans (Yes, I'm a big coffee fan!) As you walk through life each day, you're collecting beans, beans of inspiration, beans of beauty. There's beauty in the process of collecting inspiration, to be sure, but the real power comes with what you do with it.

When a coffee bean is harvested for the purposes of making coffee it goes through a few steps. It's dried, cleaned and then roasted at a high temperature. In fact, the process of pyrolysis allows the caffeol (a fragrant oil) to be released from the bean. That's what produces the flavor and aroma that many people so enjoy about coffee. Once a bean is roasted, it is then ground to prepare it for actually making the coffee. Can you see where this is going?

In much the same way, creative inspiration and ideas that we collect have to go through fire - being roasted and tested - to see which ones will remain and be worthy of further exploration. Not ever bean makes it, nor does every idea. Some need to sit for a while before they are ready. That's ok. However, the ones that are ready must be ground - pulverized - in order to be ready for the percolation process.

That pulverizing happens in the creative process. We explore, fiddle, play and refine ideas until they are worthy of further pursuit. It's there our ideas are transformed into a useable substance. The finer the grind, the stronger the coffee.

Inspiration is not the product. It is what gives birth to the product, the art. Inspiration is only a seed, much like a coffee bean. If you stop with a raw coffee bean, you'll never have coffee. If you try to make coffee from raw coffee beans it won't work. Why? The magic happens in the preparation and percolation.

The word percolate actually means to filter or trickle through. In the percolation process, the water is the solvent, and the coffee grounds are a permeable surface through which the water flows. After the beans have been harvested, dried, roasted and ground, they must be placed in a percolator to be combined with water. There's no coffee without water. When heat is applied to the bottom of the coffee pot, the water begins to boil, rising through a tube and flows out over the coffee grounds. As the water trickles down or percolates through the coffee grounds, the water-soluble compounds that give coffee it's taste, smell and texture combine with the water. Joining together, they form an entirely new substance: coffee.

During the heat of the creative process, the living water of God's presence flows through our ideas and inspiration. The water of His presence extracts the oil of anointing. It attaches to the essence of our ideas, infuses our offering with power and creates an entirely new substance for all to enjoy. That's why creating with the Holy Spirit is so transformative. Water alone does not equal coffee. Neither does a raw coffee bean. It's the percolation process that creates the transformative substance.

It's also interesting to note that in the coffee making process, you always have coffee grounds left over. Artists often become too precious with their creative process, feeling somehow, they have to include every element that inspired them during the creation of a piece. Although these elements were an important part of the process, they are not a part of the final product. To insist every part is seen only weighs down the work, making it clunky and inelegant. Just like in a painting, there are usually many unseen layers which gave you the ability to create the finished piece. As you let the creative process play out, you can be free to embrace the mystery of the unseen in your work. You can discard what's no longer needed.

Ideas for Creative Inspiration

So, what is it that inspires you? What makes your heart sing? What gives you that feeling of joy, fulfillment and connection to God like none other? Whatever it is, do it! For many prophetic artists, some inspirational activities include:

- Extended time in God's presence

- Reading God's Word
- Going to an art supply store and getting lost among the supplies
- Visiting a local museum or art exhibition
- Spending time perusing art books at a local bookstore
- Looking through Instagram or Pinterest at the work of other artists
- Taking a walk in the woods to enjoy the beauty of creation
- Daydreaming on the porch
- Gardening
- The Contemplative Practices of Imago Divina and/or Lecto Divina
- Spending time sketching ideas in your art journal

Give yourself the gift of creative space by scheduling time for yourself and your art. This can be a time where you can pull away to feed your heart - to engage in activities that draw out the creativity from your life. It can also be a time for creating in the studio, dreaming with God and being inspired in His presence.

Sometimes it's as simple as going to an art supply warehouse and browsing, visiting a museum, having an extended time of "studio time", watching a great movie, etc. Other times it can walking through the woods and enjoying the silence of the moment. Don't skimp on this! You'll be surprised when and where the Lord begins speaking to you. The most important thing is to intentionally create space for yourself to enjoy your creativity and celebrate the gift of God within you!

My Own Journey of Inspiration

I've been making baskets and woven sculpture since the mid 1990's but strangely, it's never really been about making baskets. My love for creating, my compulsion to make has always been about my passion for nature and the connection I sense when I'm engaged with it. Even as a child, I spent my days romping through the woods, collecting anything and everything that seemed interesting to me. From rocks and branches to bones and turtle shells, they all spoke to me in a special way. These beautiful natural treasures still call to me, asking me to take them to another level, combine them with other elements and celebrate their beauty. For me, creating with natural resources is a supernatural experience

When I started making baskets it was all about mastering traditional Appalachian forms, like the egg basket, using non-traditional materials like kudzu vines. Over time, my interest in other invasive plants and varied materials expanded, leading me to incorporate additional elements in my work like copper, encaustic wax, clay and more.

Since my love for nature has always been the main inspiration for my work, it was only natural my work turned in a sculptural direction in order to create nature-inspired forms. These organic and elegant creations, passion inspired sculptural works for the home, reflect the simple beauty of nature.

Be ready for the unexpected

Many times, inspiration will come as gently as a summer breeze, or as forcefully as a fireworks explosion! There are no rules. Just be ready and expectant for things like:

- Coincidences
- Visions and Internal Pictures

- A Deep Knowing or Intuition
- The Desire to Revisit a Past Creative Idea
- Words of Wisdom or Words of Knowledge

Most importantly, keep your inspirational ideas in a journal or sketchbook so you can revisit and meditate on the inspiration flowing into your life.

How God Manifests the Prophetic in an Artist

Oftentimes, artists are waiting for fireworks from Heaven, a loud booming "thus saith the Lord" or a tangible angelic visitation in their studio for their inspiration to be considered prophetic or from the Lord. Could that happen? Absolutely! But I think it's in the showing up - every day - in the studio and inviting the Holy Spirit to be a part of your process. Listening to Him as you create and responding through your creative expression is what makes your work prophetic.

I've long believed that God cares much more THAT we create than WHAT we create. You're showing up in the studio on a regular basis to do the thing God created you to do is honoring to the Lord. And you can trust God to show up, inspire you and fill your studio, your work and your life with His transformative presence.

It's not about your art being from you or God. It's neither. Rather, it's a collaborative process through which all of God moves through all of you to create unique works that reflect His heart through your artistic voice. The question is are we using our gift as intended? That's where the power, anointing and transformation are found.

How will I know if it is God or it's Me?

My friend Allen Arnold puts it this way; *"Over the years, it's become easy for me to know when the Holy Spirit is leading me in the creative process. When that is happening, it feels like a dance more than a duty. I have more joy. There's no striving or seeking validation from others. And my writing transcends me in ways I never could have made it come together.*

As a former highly-driven man, I also know what it feels like when I'm trying to do things in my own strength. I become more focused on the to-do list than walking in God's rhythm. I feel the pressure to make something happen. And my creativity lacks the eternal spark only present from co-creating with God.

Thankfully, whenever that feeling of self now tries to take over, I quickly set aside my creative project until I sense God's presence. Then I enter back into it together with Him."

This understanding of how prophetic creative expression is birthed and released should encourage you because it takes the pressure off of you to perform. Rather, you just simply cooperate with the design of God in and through your life. You don't have to be this or that, just stand as a son or daughter, receiving and stewarding that which God has entrusted to you. The more you use, practice and enlarge your gift of creating art, the more God will entrust to you. The more you're entrusted with, the more you'll see God show up in, on and through your creative expression.

Prophetic Art Calls Order Out of Chaos

Realizing everything created comes from and through the Life and Light of God, let's consider the creation account in Genesis 1:1-4:

In the beginning God created the heavens and the earth. The earth was without form, and void; and darkness was on the face of the deep. And the Spirit of God was hovering over the face of the waters. Then God said, "Let there be light"; and there was light. And God saw the light, that it was good; and God divided the light from the darkness. (NKJV)

The Spirit of God hovered over a formless dark void. The Hebrew word for hover is "rachaph" which means, "to flutter, move or shake." In the middle of this darkness God said "Let there be light," and "Let there be a release of My nature" and BOOM, that which was formless took on shape, form, and purpose. The manifestation of the Glory (or nature) of God brought transformation.

Through the finished work of Jesus Christ, we have become His image bearers--sons and daughters releasing and reflecting the nature of God through our lives and creative expression. In addition to bringing order and transformation to chaos, we are also door keepers of the presence of God.

This means we are called to release the presence of God in the earth through our creative expression and facilitate experiences where people can encounter the life and light of God as a part of their everyday existence.

Prophetic Art is Light in the Darkness

In John 1:1 we read; God is Light and Life and everything that was created was created through the Word, Jesus. Genesis 1 tells how God released his nature – Light - into the chaotic darkness and transformation occurred.

As image bearers of the Creator God, our creative expression carries His transformative nature through our prophetic voice. This process happens like everything in the Kingdom happens, by faith. For faith IS the substance or tangible evidence that the things we've seen, felt and heard in the Spirit realm are real. Our role is to bring them to the earth, to be a conduit for the mountain moving power of God to be released.

Your Creative Voice

At its most simplistic, our physical voice is made up of muscles stimulated by electrical impulses as our breath moves over them. Some people choose to train their voice to increase their vocal range so they can sing difficult patterns of notes in a variety of styles.

Well, we also have a creative voice that works the exact same way. As His *ruach* (breath) moves on, in, and through us we can move, react and create based on our developed skills.

In the scriptures, we read how Lucifer was created as an *instrument* of praise. Lucifer reflected God's Glory in his whole being, sounding forth the praise of God when he breathed. I believe we have been created with the same abilities and even more!

Your creative voice has the capacity to transmit the Life and Light of God, no matter what you do creatively. Imagine dancing and seeing people delivered from depression — making functional pottery that when used, reminds people of the goodness of God. Imagine creatively using color, form and texture in such a way that when people interact with your paintings they are healed from cancer. Imagine it. See it. For if you can see it, you can manifest it in your life with the Holy Spirit as your guide.

As you develop your 'instrument' your ability to release the Kingdom and the life of God in the earth is greatly enhanced. Skill births freedom. Freedom gives you options and the confidence to respond to the stimulation of the Spirit, allowing the breath of God to flow through your work. Don't limit the release of the Kingdom through your life, develop the gifting within you.

When you collaborate with the Holy Spirit in Kingdom creativity — His power, Life and Light merge with your faith, imaginations, and artistic skill — becoming a prophetic catalyst that carries the presence and power of God.

Art & Faith

Faith has been called the currency of Heaven. It is the way by which things get done in the Kingdom. Because faith is so foundational to our walk in the Kingdom, the Bible talks about it a lot. Consider these scriptures for a moment:

True faith must have a tangible expression.

But someone will say, "You have faith; I have deeds." Show me your faith without deeds, and I will show you my faith by what I do. — James 2:18 (NIV)

Faith is the tangible revelation of things unseen.

Now faith is the substance of things hoped for, the evidence of things not seen. — Hebrews 11:1 (NKJV)

Faith is a requirement to please God.

But without faith it is impossible to please him: for he that cometh to God must believe that he is, and that he is a rewarder of them that diligently seek him. — Hebrews 11:6 (KJV)

We are saved by grace through faith.

For it is by grace you have been saved, through faith— and this not from yourselves, it is the gift of God—not by works, so that no one can boast. For we are God's workmanship, created in Christ Jesus to do good works, which God prepared in advance for us to do. — Ephesians 2:8-10 (NIV)

By faith we become new creations (in Christ) with the capacity to transform the world by the power of the Holy Spirit working within us. As collaborators with the Holy Spirit and co-creators with the Father, we can create art that releases His Light and Life into atmospheres and situations that are dark, chaotic and void.

When I first saw the connection between art and faith, I became very excited. It's one of those things that when first discovered — your like "duh" but at the same time it's very profound.

The faith verse we're most familiar with is Hebrews 11:1: *Now faith is the substance of things hoped for, the evidence of things not seen.* (NKJV)

While meditating on this verse one day, I felt impressed by the Spirit of God to replace the word "faith" with "art" and "creativity" which made it read, "Now art or creativity is the substance of things hoped for, the evidence of things not seen." At first, the connection blew me away. Then came much fear and trembling!

The Intersection of Faith and Creativity

While meditating on this word, I began to consider the ways faith and creativity interact in the Kingdom. I started breaking it down into phrases like; *"Art is the tangible expression (the substance) of your hope and desire wrapped in your unique creative expression"* and *"Art in collaboration with the Holy*

Spirit, is the evidence (tangible expression) of the unseen realm in the earth."

The Father showed me that the essence of art and creativity is our ability to see, hear and feel things in the Spirit realm that are yet unseen in the earthly. When we see into this realm and create in collaboration with the Holy Spirit, those unseen things come into reality. This is Kingdom living!

As I meditated on this foundational truth and new revelation, I was impressed to replace the word faith in other verses-- like here in Matthew 21:21:

And Jesus answered them, "Truly, I say to you, if you have faith and do not doubt, you will not only do what has been done to the fig tree, but even if you say to this mountain, 'Be taken up and thrown into the sea,' it will happen. (ESV)

Or consider Matthew 17:20:

He said to them, "Because of your little faith. For truly, I say to you, if you have faith like a grain of mustard seed, you will say to this mountain, 'Move from here to there,' and it will move, and nothing will be impossible for you. (ESV)

This means that if your creativity is only the size of a mustard seed, your art can dislodge things that have been stuck for years…even generations! You may be thinking, what about things like depression, anxiety, sickness, disease, attacks of the enemy, or other things that I have prayed and hoped for but could not seem to get a breakthrough? Or what about really hard-hearted people who seem like they will never come to the Lord? Do you mean those things? Yes, I mean all those things.

We've all known people we've prayed for to be saved and yet nothing connects. We drag them to church, try to persuade them but nothing seems to work. Then all of a sudden, out of the blue, they call and say they got saved. When we ask how, they say something like "*Well, I was just driving down the road, minding my own business and a song came on the radio…*" How does that happen? God uses creative expression to touch their heart and affect transformation. His Spirit bypasses all the mental gymnastics in the minds of people regarding God, the Gospel and Christianity, going straight to their hearts and spirit.

The more I studied and sought the Lord on this, the more I realized God was releasing artists as prophets and Kingdom ambassadors to carry and release His power through their unique expression. Jesus used a ball of mud to heal a man's eye. The Apostle Paul prayed over a simple cloth and sent it to the sick as a point of contact for healing. Likewise, God uses artists songs, paintings, dances, books and poetry to carry the Light and Life of God to bring transformation to the environments they inhabit.

Creativity carries the ability to 'move mountains' because it carries God's Light and Life and is a powerful tool in the hands of God's sons and daughters. This is why the enemy works overtime to steal, kill and destroy Kingdom artists and thwart their impact on the earth. Since creativity is a gift freely given to people by God, it can be used for the

Glory of God or for the glory of man. Creativity will always produce fruit based on its root. However, it can be brought to full maturity when seated in the humble heart of a man or woman who is crucified with Christ and risen in Him.

Stewarding the Gift of Creativity

There is a parable found in Matthew 25 known as The Parable of the Talents. Three men were entrusted with money to invest while their master was away. Two invested the money they were given, but one man hid his money in the ground. He didn't lack the ability to earn an investment, but had a problem believing he could. He told the master of the field "*I knew you to be a hard man...*" In other words, I believed I couldn't live up to your standards, so I didn't even try.

My friend, what you believe about yourself and who God is determines your possibilities.

Just like the men in the Parable of the Talents, you are I are responsible for the revelation God entrusts to us. It's literally a Kingdom investment the Father has placed inside of you, and He waits to see what you will do with it. That investment has the ability to grow, produce, multiply and expand when mixed with faith or it can sit dormant. The more you enlarge your capacity for his presence by becoming excellent at what you do, the more the father will entrust to you. That's how you grow in the Kingdom.

My friend, artist Phillip Ortiz shared a story of how his art released the Light and Life of God in the most unlikely way:

"About 4 years ago a friend invited me to be a part of an art outreach team she was forming in downtown Kansas City. Kansas City hosts a robust event called First Fridays in the Summer. It includes vendors, music concerts, food and beer. The streets are filled with people of all walks of life. It's not really a "family friendly" event, but thousands of people come. She had the crazy idea to give out prophetic words through our art in 5–10 minute increments (talk about pressure, we created over 300 pieces that year).

We set up in front of a high-end art gallery. The manager came out to ask what we were doing. Upon realizing we had permission, she was annoyed but asked the nature of the art we were creating. I explained how we asked God to give us an image for the people who came and then created it for them. I explained to her that God is always speaking, and we just have to listen. I asked if she wanted one and she smirked but said yes. I told her if what I saw was not accurate, she could write-me-off as crazy. Since she had to get back to work, I told her I would go find her when I was done. I asked her her name and then asked God what He wanted to say to her. Immediately I saw an image of a potted plant that had split in two then mended. I saw scissors cut the cloth that had been used for the mending. So, I sketched it out. The Lord showed me her heart was hurting deeply because of family tensions, loss and pain, but that He wanted to mend her heart.

When I shared it with her, she began to cry. She explained she had recently lost her husband and was overwhelmed by the loss. She was having quite a bit of relational tension in her work and in her family. She then told me she was a passionate gardener, and her favorite thing was to care for and mend plants. At this point I was crying too... mind blown, heart alive. God won the lady over. Though I never saw her again, several months later my friend said she had come by the art booth to say she had told EVERYONE who worked in the gallery, including her boss, how the little 10-minute sketch "gallery-framed her".

The Process of Creating Prophetic Art

As you sense God's presence and hear the nuances of His Spirit, respond. God desires to meet with you in your studio. If you'll simply open the door--trust me-- He will come in! The key is simply to get into the studio and start working in faith! Believe that as you create, God is creating with You.

Artist Yoonsoo Nam describes her process this way, saying *"The Holy Spirit is gentle and kind. He never controls me but leads me when I open my heart to Him. He is like water that continues to drench me and fills me up. Also, He is so powerful and mighty. He is like fire that purifies my heart and empowers me to create something new. When He moves in me and through me, there is no effort needed to create something. It just flows. The more I yield to Him, More I experience His creative excellence. I cannot do anything apart from Him. However, when I become one with Him, I am free in His Spirit and the supernatural boldness, creativity, wisdom, understanding come and possess me."*

My own studio is not just a place I work but rather an incubator where materials and ideas converge. It is a place of experimentation where ideas are forged and creations come to life. As I enter the creative process, often I don't even have an idea of what I'm going to create. I spend time in worship and with my materials. I look through sketchbooks, play with shapes and textures. For me, the studio is a sacred space where divine inspiration overshadows skillful hands and art is born. I don't wait for inspiration to come upon me, I trust it's already within me. Inspiration emerges in the context of the creative process. Trusting the process is important, even when you don't understand everything going on while you're creating.

What Tools Are in Your Hand?

As you think about your own unique Kingdom design, what is it the Father has given you? Maybe it's:

- An idea
- A resource
- A tool
- A talent
- Or even a relationship

Take these things and begin to steward them. Stretch, build, grow and enhance what you have in order to enlarge your capacity to create and move with the Spirit of God.

The Prophetic "Chipping Away"

My friend Ray Hughes has often said ideas that come from God are like diamonds in lumps of coal. There's a lot of potential beauty inside but much has to be chipped away and polished before it can be realized.

What are the next steps you need to take to see that diamond begin to come forth and shine? Is there something that needs to be chipped away?

All artists and Kingdom creatives are on a journey of personal development. This is why we need operate prophetically in our creative process, so we can sense where to move and what to do next. It's encouraging to know we are not alone in the process.

The Process of Uncovering

Almost every artist goes through difficult seasons, seasons when the work no longer resonates with their spirit. They begin to thrash around, not knowing where to go, what to pursue or what direction is next. It's a very frustrating yet necessary part of evolving as a creative. Yet that very frustration can often be the catalyst we need to step out of our comfort zone and press into new realms of creativity.

I remember this season vividly as I wrestled with my work, wondering why I was doing basketry in the first place. During this season, I went back to the basics and rediscovered my love for natural materials, harvesting and the beauty of how things work together. Memories rushed back. Walks in the woods. Trips to the western coast of Scotland. Australian pods. Nests and river rocks. Soon, everything I saw looked like a basket and that's when things started to change.

Along my journey of rediscovery. 19th century Japanese ikebana baskets became a major source of inspiration, particularly how makers attached randomly woven nest-like baskets into knarly wisteria roots. The first one I saw on Pinterest literally made me cry; it evoked such deep emotion. For me, basketry ceased to be defined by techniques and functional forms. I began to see it as a language for my unique creative expression. Now, instead of just using nature as a source of materials for weaving, I was digging deeper. Nature became my source of inspiration and I'm still loving the process.

The Bible says in Proverbs 25:2 that "*It is the glory of God to conceal a matter, But the glory of kings is to search out a matter.*" (NKJV) I sense God's pleasure and participate with Him in the creative process as I dream, dig, uncover, stretch and create. Life is about movement. As I continue to make art that resonates with the glory of nature, I lean into the fact that everything moves, lives, breathes and exists within the breath of the Creator. God is glorified and I am fulfilled when I create with Him. I realize the forest has captured my heart. No longer can I make things that have no spirit, reveal no life. I must resonate with the One who created all things and who also created me. I must reveal and reflect Him and the glory of His creation.

I Am a Maker

I was made to be a maker
With busy hands and thoughts and dreams.
I see the things that no one else sees
And wonder why not me.
I begin in places not understood
Just to end in places of unexpected joy.
I dream of beauty yet manifested
And wake to craft the wind.
I hear the sounds of life blowing through ideas
As I quiet my soul and quicken my hands
To make, create and release the dreams
Of the One who dreams with me.
I am a Maker.

Revelation & Imagination

When a creative idea begins to percolate, it will usually come as some sort of inspiration. Maybe you see, know, hear, smell or sense something that catches your attention and you become inspired. It may be a place, a person, a song or a natural setting that you see every day or something that you've encountered for the first time. Regardless of how it happens, at that moment you have an encounter. The Spirit speaks and you have an "Ah-ha" moment – a light bulb experience where you know you need to pay attention. Your willingness to sense and respond to that revelation is foundational in your ability to move prophetically in the creative process. There is no art without your response.

The Art of Imagination

Google Dictionary defines imagination as *the faculty or action of forming new ideas, or images; concepts of external objects not present to the senses.*

Our imagination is a God-designed engine that receives impulses, desires and information from the Holy Spirit, ourselves, others and the world around us. It then formulates images, concepts and ideas based on the beliefs in our hearts.

The Latin root word for imagination is *imaginari* which means *to picture oneself.* Our imagination engine mixes with our faith and creates pictures, stories and movies. These images create desire within the heart. The heart then acts as an incubator, a seedbed or a womb to bring the images and concepts into reality. In fact, in Strong's Concordance, "yetser", which is often translated as imagination or intention in the Bible, comes from the root word, "yatsar". This powerful word means to form or fashion like a potter would earthenware. In fact, one of the meanings of this word happens to be conception. How incredible that God has designed our imagination to form, develop and give birth to His ideas through us as we co-labor with the Holy Spirit! It's the place there the seeds of inspiration sprout and bear fruit for God's Glory.

Your imagination is an internal place where God interacts with you through the power of the Holy Spirit. It is a gift to every person ever created and gives you the ability to dream, to see and know before you actually create. Imagination is foundational for every believer. Without it, the faith process gets derailed. And just like every gift given by the Father to humanity, it has to be submitted to the Lordship of Jesus and set apart for His Glory.

Imagination is the First Step

Imagining is where the creative process begins for most artists. For the believer, our imagination has the capacity to interact with the Holy Spirit in our human spirit and is then processed through our soul and body. It takes all the inspiration, experiences and understanding we currently have and mixes it together with all our dreams of what could be. It creates an inner vision inside of us by which we create from. And as we walk with the Lord, we can trust that vision and intuitions are both from Him and for us. Vision fuels our creative process even when we don't yet fully understand how it will manifest.

This ability to see that which is not as though it already is, is the nature of God manifested through us. To imagine and see what is the highest, best expression of His Glory through our lives and creativity. Without a clear vision on the inside, it's very difficult to function creatively or in the Kingdom for that matter. Remember, that's why the Bible says in Proverbs 29:18 that people tend to perish or cast off restraint when there is a lack of vision or prophetic revelation. This is why the enemy is all about lying to, confusing and ultimately trying to conquer our mind. He wants to replace God's vision with lies to alter our perception of what's possible.

The Pictures Inside You

Paul talked about this as he encouraged early believers to mature in their relationship with the Father. The first mention is in Romans 12:2: *"Do not conform to the pattern of this world, but be transformed by the renewing of your mind. Then you will be able to test and approve what God's will is--his good, pleasing and perfect will."* (NIV) In other words, don't think like the world thinks, don't hold their vision of reality and possibility in your mind and heart, instead renew your mind with God's Truth, which brings Kingdom transformation.

His second mention is in 2 Corinthians 10:3-5 (KJV) where he exhorts the church: *"For though we walk in the flesh, we do not war after the flesh: (For the weapons of our warfare are not carnal, but mighty through God to the pulling down of strong holds;) Casting down (vain) imaginations, and every high thing that exalteth itself against the knowledge of God, and bringing into captivity every thought to the obedience of Christ."*

Paul knew the importance of guarding our internal Spirit breathed images, images holding godly transformative power. Satan's destructive lies can only bring death and should have no place within the mind of the believer. Left to germinate, his images will bear ungodly fruit. We must cultivate this incredible creative engine within us, not dismiss it to the sidelines of our life in the Kingdom.

Prophetic Imagination & the Kingdom Within

Our human spirit and the process of imagining, connect us to the Kingdom within. Instead of connecting to our rule and reign, or as Paul says *the pattern of this world*, we connect to the rule and reign of the divine Kingdom that lives inside of us through the cross of Jesus and power of the Holy Spirit. That's how we prophetically bring heaven's reality and nature to the earth. This process of imagining is not only crucial to our creative process but to our whole life because creativity and living a life of passion and abundance are directly connected.

Our ability to imagine is vital to creating and demonstrating the Kingdom and is tied to your acceptance of God's purposes established in you through Christ. You are a son and daughter in His Kingdom.

Sometimes God will give us a visual example like He did with Abram in Genesis 15 (God compared the stars of the sky to his descendants) or ignite our heart toward an expected outcome like he did with Mary, the mother of Jesus in Luke 1 (The angel gave her a visual picture of what was to come). And other times we produce the images of possibility with our imagination. I think that's what David did.

David was a lover of God and a worshipper. Firm in that identity; dreams, visions and promises probably began to take root in His heart. As He mixed his faith with the vision of what he saw as possible – daily worship providing unlimited access to the Father – things began to happen. Doors opened. People began to respond and affirm His purpose. Eventually David became King and established what we now know as the Tabernacle of

David – a center of 24/7 worship involving thousands of musicians and creatives for over 30 years. Did this all happen just because God wanted it that way? No, it was because God found a man who would dream with Him and release His nature in the earth by engaging his imagination. Transformation was the result. It can be the same in your life and art.

Strengthen Your Imagination

There are some practical ways to strengthen your imagination. Pray in the Spirit, ask God for pictures, meditate on His Word and specifically His promises regarding your identity and your purpose. Spend time in worship, soaking in His presence. Cultivate hearing His voice within you. Participate in activities that bring you life; a walk in the woods, creating art or daydreaming on the porch. As you give yourself mental and emotional space to breathe, pictures will begin to form. Thank God for them as they float into your mind. Meditate on them in your imagination. Mix your faith with the picture and the promises of God. Then, watch God begin to bring it forth through you as you cooperate with Him.

The Power of Agreement & Response

Agreement is a powerful law in the Kingdom of God. In fact, it's like the law of gravity. Regardless of how you use it - for good or for evil - it works, every time. You're probably used to applying this law on a regular basis in your art without knowing it. When you have an idea, you either say yes, thinking it's a great idea and decide to pursue that or you think, no, I don't think I can do that, it seems too hard. Either way, you're right. The artists who agree with Holy Spirit inspiration - regardless of whether or not they feel qualified - are the ones who will begin to create prophetic art with Him.

Life or Death

Agreement opens the door and gives whatever you agree with access to move in your life. You'll always eat the fruit of that which you agree. Let's look at some negative examples of agreement and how they resulted in death, rather than life:

- Adam and Eve agreed with the devil rather than God, reaping a curse upon their life and eternal separation from God.
- Cain agreed with the jealousy and rage in his heart, killing his brother and ultimately living a life of wandering and striving.
- The people in the Tower of Babel story wanted to build a tower to heaven, but ultimately were destroyed because of their rebellion.

Notice what God says of agreement here in the Tower of Babel story:

"And the LORD said, "Behold, they are one [unified] people, and they all have the same language. This is only the beginning of what they will do [in rebellion against

Me], and now no evil thing they imagine they can do will be impossible for them." Genesis 11:6 (AMP)

That's pretty amazing! God said nothing would be impossible for them when they were in agreement. A powerful, but potentially dangerous principle.

Now consider these incredible examples from God's Word that show us the fruit of godly agreement:

- Noah agreed with the promise of God and was saved from destruction. After the flood, he and his family were used to restore and replenish the earth.
- Moses agreed with God's calling on his life even though he felt unworthy. It opened the door to freedom for a whole nation.
- Jesus agreed with the divine will of His Father and went to the cross, resulting in the redemption and restoration of all humanity.

Jesus is clearly teaching about the principle of agreement when He said:

"Again, I give you an eternal truth: If two of you agree to ask God for something in a symphony of prayer, my heavenly Father will do it for you. For wherever two or three come together in honor of my name, I am right there with them!" - Matthew 18:19-21 (TPT)

If the law of agreement works in both a negative and positive context, imagine what would happen when we agree with God! Instead of trying to make things happen through striving or natural knowledge, we can open the door for Heaven's divine creativity to flow through us.

Art is a Response

Creating with the Holy Spirit is not just imagining what could be. It's imagining followed by stepping out in the context of our creative expression. We need to see and agree. See what God is showing, sense what He's doing, feel where He's moving, hear what He's saying and then give it our YES! When we create based on the revelation and inspiration we receive, we manifest the life of God.

Responding to inspiration becomes easier as we become both filled and skilled. It's a two-winged plane that must function together for "maximum lift". Otherwise, we'll nose dive creatively and spiritually.

Exodus 31 describes how being both filled and skilled is God's ideal for artists. When all of you is filled with all of God, you will do the things God inspires you to do through your unique gifting and artistic skills. Being filled and skilled is all about operating at your fullest capacity in the midst of a divine tension. Filled with the Spirit of God and leveraging all the skill you have to release His Glory through your expression. This divine tension creates the resonance with which our artistic voices are expressed!

Growth in the Kingdom of God happens when you lean in into this concept. I believe it to be a foundational concept in God's Kingdom, not just for artists, but for every person wanting to thrive in all God has for him. It's just not enough to be filled with the Spirit and sit around, enjoying the glory of His presence. As wonderful and vital as that is in our life, it should lead us out of our comfort zones and ourselves. As we grow in His presence, we must also lean into skill development, because that enlarges our capacity to be carriers of His presence and steward well the gifts, talents, callings, and opportunities that God gives us. Without a beautiful balance, we run around in circles either full of passion but lacking skill or extremely skilled with no life. It's a balanced collaboration between God and man, and in no way diminishes the supernatural component of how God works in our life.

If you're like me, you've probably had times in your life when you asked God to just supernaturally download something so you could get on with it, knowing He could absolutely do that, but more than likely it didn't happen that way. Not because God doesn't love you, but because He's all about the process of walking with us on the journey. He has invested something in you, and He wants to lead, guide, and inspire you with every day opportunities so you come to know the intimate beauty of walking with Him.

As we faithfully walk this journey out — increase and fruitfulness can be ours. That's just how the Kingdom works.

If we only see in the Spirit without expressing what we see, we'll end up frustrated because hope (a vision of what could be) deferred makes the heart sick. On the other hand, we can go through a bunch of lifeless motions but unless there's a clear picture in your heart and mind of what's possible, mixed with faith, we're going nowhere fast.

Suffice it to say, there has to be a constant infilling of the Holy Spirit through our intimate relationship with Jesus. Being continually filled (Ephesians 5:18) prompts our desires, dreams, passion and pictures. It affirms your identity and causes you to triumph. It anchors you in the truth of God's Kingdom.

A Skillful Response is Required

At the same time "faith without works is dead." God initiates and we respond based on our current skill set. As you grow in your relationship with Christ and allow the Holy Spirit to fill you, you must also grow in your skills. Giving attention to both as led by the Spirit of God produces maturity and brings you into a place of increase.

If we want to have a seat at the table of influence and become a conduit of Kingdom transformation, we must pursue, acquire and master artistic skill. As we diligently pursue our own artistic development, the Bible is clear in Proverbs 18:16 when it says *"A man's gift make's room for him and brings him before great men."* (NKJV) If you want to see your art become a conduit for influence and impact, hone your skills.

Art as Incarnation

If imagination is our source and Spirit-led execution is the process, then art is the product. Your art, or whatever your creative expression happens to be, brings into reality that which up until this point has only been a hope. By its very nature, the act of creating is incarnational because it brings forth the purpose and promise of God to the earth in tangible form. In this incarnational process, what was once only a dream now becomes a tangible reality carrying the life and light of God!

Artist Karen Swenholt shared with me how her work became the incarnation of God's presence for her viewers; *"My gallery owner reported a visitor who saw my Biblical narrative sculpture called, "The Hem of*

His Garment." As the gallery director shared the story behind the sculpture, the woman declared, "I am the woman!" She had been deeply involved in New Age thought. The sculpture and subsequent discussions with me and my gallery owner were her first exposure to Christianity.

At another 'retrospective' art opening, a woman broke into tears while viewing "Counselor." The piece is based on my mother's difficulty with forgiveness. Because of my mother's religious upbringing, she had no exposure to the concept. The woman was raised by a bitter mother who also had problems with forgiveness. I explained the piece and we prayed together right there at the opening reception for the woman's emotional healing."

This incarnational process is a core part of God's divine nature. When we participate in His divine nature - through faith in His precious promises - we then become participants in the incarnation, bringing the divine into the earth realm for all to see, interact with and be transformed by.

Artist, Ashley Rogers shared a story of how God is using her in this incarnational process: *"As an art ministry, God gave us connections to some amazing people in our beautiful vibrant city, San Antonio. Because of our nearness to the border of Mexico, there are thousands of immigrants in our city that have walked through intense trauma, and a vast majority do not speak English. Art has been an amazing way to breakthrough these language barriers and allow the Holy Spirit to speak, move and heal. Sometimes we face paint the cheeks of children that are simply needing a fun, childish normal experience. Other times it looks like offering simple coloring books and markers. I am always amazed how the adults are just as drawn in to coloring with a crayon. One ministry that we work alongside ministers directly to women that are fleeing trauma in other countries and looking for a new life. I was asked to reflect on the trauma process that often occurs and turn it into a painting that could help visually illustrate where the women are at. Art has the power to quickly identify our deepest felt emotions. It's a beautiful gift. The director of the ministry now uses the painting when women come in, and they point to the part they can best identify with. Not only does it quickly illuminate where they are in their healing journey (such as "fight" or "flight") but it also allows them to visually see themselves in their pain, but with the hope of healing by God in sight."*

The Kingdom is Established through Sons & Daughters

My friend, Jason Leith who is an artist in southern California and Visual Arts Pastor at Saddleback Church shared a story of transformation with me that is so powerful. While working on portraits for a public art installation project he was leading called Sacred Streets[1], featuring twelve portraits of individuals who were living on the streets of Skid Row, a man asked Jason to create a portrait of him as well. Even though Jason had finished, his assignment, he took the time to connect with this man and draw his portrait using simple charcoal and large discarded scraps of cardboard. As Jason drew,

---

[1] Find out more at www.SacredStreets.org

the two had a meaningful conversation about life, identity and the traumatic events that all humans walk through including violence and a lifetime of addiction.

After completing the basics of the portrait, Jason showed the sketch to the man and then had to leave. He took the sketch with him so he could complete it, later. But when Jason returned ten days later to reveal the finished piece, Robert was nowhere to be found. Even when he asked around, nobody knew where he was, which was very unusual. Later that day, Robert called Jason to let him know that the sketch Jason had done of him helped him truly see himself for the first time and he had checked himself into a rehab center to begin his recovery journey. Wow! Now that is Kingdom transformation.

For me, this is where the rubber meets the road. Regardless of our unique gifting or calling, the Kingdom of God is established as sons and daughters release demonstrations of Kingdom reality into the culture. Jesus promised that we would do greater works than He did, that signs and wonders would follow those who believe in Him. My friend, your creative expression was destined, from the very foundation of the earth, to be the incarnated demonstration of God's Kingdom.

Abundance is the Fruit of Transformation

The result of Kingdom transformation is always life, especially when it comes through the creative expression of sons and daughters. Life abundant. Life everlasting. Life rooted and grounded in love. Transformation equals abundance. When God's abundance overflows, it activates the dormant places in the heart causing vision, purpose and desire to spring forth. Man fully alive, fully satisfied in God, fully loved by God and fully able to stand in His Kingdom purpose. But it's not a stopping point! Instead, it's the ground where abundant life (John 10:10) is experienced and new inspiration is birthed.

Abundance is a prophetic Kingdom demonstration of the world to come. A display of the New Creation. As we create with the Holy Spirit, He infuses the artist and the art, feeding our souls, filling our senses and drawing us into the divine dance of creativity. Both in times of joy and sorrow, plenty and need, art becomes a vehicle to experience and communicate the abundance of the Kingdom. Our art and the very process of making it becomes a place of solace and joy, life and comfort.

What we create with the Holy Spirit matters both now and for eternity. We are participating in God's eternal story through the work we create and the lives we live. Our work gives voice, word, image and emotion to the promise of God's new reality in the Kingdom.

Cooperation, Not Performance

Abundance and creativity always manifest in our life when we come into alignment with the intention or design of God for our life, whether as co-creators or ones interacting with the Spirit-birthed creation. This doesn't mean we'll never have another problem in our life or that grace is some ticket to easy street. It does mean, however, that worry is no longer an option because at the end of the day, you know you are secure, provided for, and in the Beloved of Almighty God. Otherwise, we stay frustrated in the ego portion of our being - our soul, mind will, emotions - wrestling with feelings of inadequacy, powerlessness and frustration.

Consider this story by artist Antonia Ruppert, who shared a recent encounter with me; "*God has used my art to connect people. I realized how transforming this was one afternoon during a community art event. I'd been painting for a while when several people brought an older woman up to the canvas. She seemed to light up and started painting with the supplies provided. After a while, the people with her told me that she had not been able to paint since immigrating to the United States. This was a powerful moment for her to do something she loved--with freedom. I was awestruck in the moment that God would lead her to my event.*"

And then there's my friend, artist Brian Peterson, who leads an incredible ministry called Faces of Santa Ana[2] out in California. They serve people

---

[2] Find out more at www.FacesofSantaAna.com

struggling with homelessness through art and personal relationships. He shared a powerful story of creative abundance with me: *"Recently, I painted a portrait of my neighbor Dana who is experiencing homelessness. Upon sharing his portrait with him, Dana exclaimed, 'I look confident!'. This did not seem like a huge moment on the outside, but something was changing in the inner depths of Dana's heart. Two days later, Dana came to my front door ready to share his good news. He had reconnected with his homeless services case manager and would receive housing in the coming days through a mental health program. These support resources were there all along, but it was only when Dana saw himself through the lens of confidence that he believed he was worthy to run after them. A seed of confidence in his heart turned into small actions that led to big results."*

When we become ambassadors of abundance, the supernatural flow of Heaven moves through us.

Artist Sonja Kreisel is a dancer, painter and worship flag artist. She shared a recent story of a healing that took place through her art with me; "*My husband and I held our first workshop together teaching about creative worship with flags in a church. In the workshop was a lady who had just suffered a lung infection. She was not sure if she was able to participate fully, as she was still very short of breath. As she was dancing with our flags, she felt her lungs open up and experienced full healing and restoration of her lung function. When she asked what the specific names of the flags, she had danced with were, I realized they were called `New breath´. Not only did this lady experience healing for her lungs but her long laid aside call and desire for dance and worship dance got reignited! She started dancing in church again and teaching the kids there too.*" Wow! Praise God for His abundant healing flow!

When pondering on my own creative process and how I interact with the Holy Spirit, I penned this poetic reflection called "*On Creating*". I hope it will inspire and encourage you as you continue on your journey of creating with the creator!

On Creating

It has been said that all creativity happens at the edge of chaos and order…

For me the chaos just happens to look like tangled, gnarly vines wrapped tightly around strangled trees and laurel, pods and cones littering the forest floor; the order like a beautiful sculptural basket that reminds me of its source.

Somewhere in the middle is where the magic happens, where Creativity broods over the chaos and new life begins; beauty is born.

A simple walk through the forest explodes into a symphony of possibilities; back breaking in giddy glee as I carry the treasures toward their purpose. What once was dead is now alive, that which was hated is now desired, that which had no breath suddenly heaves with hope afresh.

The weaving is the easy part; it's seeing beauty while it's still hidden that is the adventure. Even though these woven creations seem to simply form in the hands of their maker, as if to say it is only skill that brings them to life, it must always be remembered that every basket begins with a walk in the woods.

It's time to take a walk.

Matt Tommey Copyright 2014

Glory Stories of God's Transforming Power

The transformational power of art created through the hands of Spirit-led artists is without question. All over the world, God is using artists to release His transforming power through their art. Like artist Nathan Rhoads, who shared a story of healing through his art; *"While painting at a revival conference, I created a piece about revival in the area, and what God was wanting to release regionally. After I finished painting, two women came up to chat with me about the painting. As we were chatting, one of the women told me that she had polyps in her throat and that as she looked at the painting, her polyps dissolved. My mind was blown away. I had created a painting about revival, and somehow God healed this woman. All three of us were amazed at what God did."*

And artist, Linda Harris Lorio, who shared a story from a recent conference she painted at; *"I was painting live on stage at a Christian conference in Wisconsin. I painted a young woman rising up and dancing out of the "dead dry bones" of her past. I painted a cross on her wrist. I revealed and explained the painting on stage. A young woman came up and showed me a cross tattoo on her wrist. The tattoo was covering deep cut marks. She explained she was a "cutter". She would cut her wrists and arms. The cuts on her wrist were right where I had painted a cross on the wrist in my painting. She received prayer and deliverance that night. The girl in the painting even looked like her."*

Prophetic psalmist, Tammy Sorenson, shared; *"A young girl around the age of five came to me via her grandmother. She had been severely abused during her first year of life and anorexia had become the one thing she could control. I met with them both at our church and in the context of sound therapy sessions. This young girl encountered Jesus and the Holy Spirit during our time of worship while my music played over her. Everything profoundly and suddenly changed. This young girl discovered she had a prophetic gifting to write, to sing, and to pray. She has blossomed into a vibrant confident and anointed teenager in love with Jesus. They play my music in their home 24/7 and have many personal testimonies to share."*

My friend, artist Theresa Dedmon, sees healing and transformation through her art on a regular basis. She said *"I see miracles happen because I make room for Him to do the impossible through what I create. One time I was speaking at Randy Clark's School of Ministry in Pennsylvania and felt like God wanted to heal people from night terrors. A person stood up and I gave them my art piece to look at before they went to bed. I found out later that they were completely healed!*

The following year, I was picked up at the airport to speak at Randy's school again, and the person who picked me up told me more of the story. This woman was an online student the year before and her husband had dealt with night terrors every night for 25 years. She had asked the student who had received the art piece from me the year before to text her the painting I had done for her.

She told me her husband would look at this painting on his phone every night and had never had a nightmare again! God is good! I have seen miracles happen instantaneously as people with pain in different parts of their body look at my art. I have seen the pain leave! God's heart is for people to be healed and restored and our art has an anointing through our co-creating with God to release healing, just as the demon left Saul when David played his instrument in I Samuel 16. All it takes is risk, co-creating with God, and releasing what He shows you to create!"

My dear friend, artist Mayra Pankow from Germany shared this testimony from a couple she created a painting for as they went through IVF. They said *"My husband and I wanted to have a baby for 5 years. Despite various medical examinations and treatments, unfortunately, it was always unsuccessful. After our second unsuccessful IVF treatment, we were very helpless as to whether to try again. When we decided to try a third time, Mayra began to paint pictures for us.*

Again and again, sometimes every day, she sent me pictures and encouraging words. Although many people prayed for us, Mayra's prayers and pictures were very special. When I was hopeless or when I was afraid (especially at night) I would look at the pictures again and again, proclaiming their prayers. This helped me a lot, especially when I couldn't find my own words. Although we never saw each other physically during this time, I felt very connected to Mayra. And the great miracle: God answered our prayers! I became pregnant with our baby. The pregnancy had many complications, but the pictures and promises from Mayra always helped me to hold on to hope." How beautiful! She even went on to report that the baby was born healthy, strong and doing well!

Artist Bryn Gillette shared this story *"When we first began having children, some dear friends were over at our house holding our newborn son. They were in tears because of the pain they were experiencing as they struggled to get pregnant. I felt prompted to paint a blessing for them and did a painting of 'mother Lisa' holding our son. I really created it as a prayer over her future as a mother. Just weeks after giving her the work they excitedly shared they were pregnant, and that work still hangs in their son's bedroom."*

Artist Isabel Castaneda shared a story with me about giving a painting away that become a prophetic confirmation for a missionary couple to adopt a child. *"I remember when I gave a copy of my painting 'Mother and Child' to a missionary couple who came to visit my church about 13 years ago. When they saw the painting, they were so touched and almost in tears because they were praying about adopting a little girl from Guatemala. My painting was of a Guatemalan mom carrying her child on her back. They received that as a confirmation and planned to move forward with the adoption."*

Remember, God is no respecter of persons. If He is releasing transformation through the lives and art of these artists, He is ready and willing to do the same for you! Simply begin to invite Him into your process, expect His Spirit to lead you and start creating. There's no pressure. The results are up to

Him! Just like the boy with the loaves and fish in Matthew 14, all you have to do is bring what you have to offer. Jesus is the multiplier and accelerator.

Pray this prayer with me:

Father, I thank you for the invitation to create with You. I know if you worked through these artists, you will work through me, too! Thank you that you designed me specifically as an artist to release your Light and Life to the world. Thank you that your Holy Spirit lives inside me. I am not alone, forsaken or forgotten. I am your beloved and have everything I need to thrive as the artist you created me to be. I believe you have plans to prosper me and I come into agreement with those plans now. Give me faith to walk with you even when I can't see the whole picture. I trust that as I create with you, you will use me for your glory. I release all the stress and performance anxiety of perfectionism right now in the name of Jesus. I welcome your freedom and commit my ways to you in Jesus' name, trusting that you will cause me to thrive like an oak planted by the waters of life. I love you, Lord and by faith, I receive every good thing you have for me. Amen.

Matt Tommey

FAQ's about Prophetic Art

I've had the great privilege of helping thousands of artists over the years flow in their prophetic gifting. Here are the answers to some of their most common questions:

Is every artist prophetic?

Not every artist approaches their work with a prophetic intention i.e.: to be inspired by and create with the Holy Spirit in order to be used by God to release His Life and Light to the world. However, God is sovereign, and He often chooses to use the foolish things - like art - to confound the wise.

Because God can speak in and through anything He chooses, He often uses the "unholy" for "holy" purposes. You've probably experienced that before, right? A random song comes on the radio and boom, out of nowhere the Holy Spirit is speaking to you in the context of that song. Did the artist intend for that to happen? Probably not. Did God use it in your life and in that moment, it became prophetic? Absolutely. This is the mystery of the creative process. As we are faithful to create with Holy Spirit, He chooses to use our work as He will in the lives of those who interact with it.

Is prophetic art only for painters?

Absolutely not! Over the last 15 years, I've seen a significant rise in the number of artists who consider themselves to be prophetic artists. While painters have primarily been the forerunners and have brought attention to the arts within the Body of Christ again, that's only part of the story. Every artist has the ability to approach their work from a prophetic intention. Poets and potters, weavers and writers, jewelers and mixed media artists, sculptors and seamstresses, dancers and musicians all have a part to play in the tapestry of God's beautiful Kingdom.

What's the difference between worship art and prophetic art?

Most of the time, these phrases are used synonymously. However, I would like to draw a distinction here. Worship Art most often refers to art that's being created in the context of corporate worship. For example, a painter on stage as a part of a worship team during a worship service. In that context, any artistic expression in corporate worship could be considered worship art i.e.: a potter throwing on the wheel, a group of dancers or even a spoken word artist.

Prophetic Art is a much larger term speaking to the *intention* of the artist to create with the Holy Spirit and does not have to be in the context of corporate worship. To blur the lines even further, I would suggest that all prophetic art is worship art because as we create it is an act of worship before the Lord — an intentional offering meant to glorify God and inspire others toward the same. As Ray Hughes said in the foreword of my book "Unlocking the Heart of the Artist":

"I believe "worship happens when you sense an acute awareness of the presence of God, and God senses an acute awareness of the presence of you." Because those moments are so precious, they should be fully lived. Those moments should become songs, poems, and works of art. They should be dances, sculptures, paintings, carvings, pottery, etc. By bringing our creativity into the atmosphere of worship to our creator, we have the ability to expand the atmosphere and extend or magnify our worship."

Is it ok to sell prophetic art or God-inspired art since I feel God gave me the inspiration?

Absolutely and here are the reasons why:

First of all, 1 Timothy 5:18 says:

"For the Scripture says, "You shall not muzzle the ox while it is treading out the grain [to keep it from eating]," and, "The worker is worthy of his wages [he deserves fair compensation]." (AMP)

In other words, if you're doing the work, you deserve to be paid. Rarely does this question arise in a business setting. Unfortunately, because the arts have a history of being "volunteered" in the church (at least within the Protestant tradition of the last

500 years) there can be an expectation you should donate your work because it is God inspired.

First of all, that's a fundamental misunderstanding of how provision flows in the Kingdom of God. In the Kingdom, God brings our provision to us in the context of our assignment. As you embrace your unique design in God's Kingdom and trust Him as your provider, the Holy Spirit will lead you in how to find and gather the provision God has for you in line with your specific Kingdom assignment. If your calling is as an artist, then you can trust God wants to bring your provision through that calling. The more you steward your calling and the resources He brings you, the more you'll receive as you continue on your journey.

The marketplace provides opportunities for artists to both make a living from and share their art with people who are willing to invest in their creative expression. Financial provision allows an artist the time and freedom to focus on their art making journey. For everyone in the Kingdom, God releases ideas that generate money in the marketplace.

Secondly, this question arises because many artists who consider their work and art process to be prophetic only show their work in the context of their local church. Your work can bless the church - and should - but it's meant for the marketplace. Determine in your heart whether the art your creating is ministry (willing to give it away) or if it is your business (you are paid a market rate for what you create). There's no right or wrong, but it's important for you to draw that distinction for yourself and others so there's no unmet expectations or misunderstandings.

There is also confusion when considering what season of life an artist is in. I wrote an in-depth article on my blog called "Considering Art as Spiritual Experience, Hobby and Vocation". This might be helpful if you're wrestling with knowing what season of life you're in and how you want to share your art.

Is prophetic art always an exact representation of specific visions, dreams or impressions?

No, quite the contrary. I'm convinced that much of what we've seen so far in the prophetic art movement is an immature expression of a mature inspiration. In an effort to be true to the inspiration (and what the artist feels is God's heart) they often try to capture the dream, vision or idea representationally rather than asking deeper questions like: what does this mean on a deeper level, how does this inspire me to seek further information, what are atypical ways I could explore this subject to inspire thought and curiosity? Remember, all creativity, whether representational or abstract, functional or purely aesthetic, can be both inspired and used by the Holy Spirit for His transformational purposes in the artist and the viewer.

I feel the pressure to be perfect when creating art considered to be "prophetic". Is there a right way and a wrong way to create prophetic art?

I really believe Christian artists should quit trying so hard to 'say something' with their art and simply create. Create with skill, from deep inspiration *with* the Creator. Just create and believe me, the work will speak for itself.

So many times overt "Christainese" messages overwhelm and weaken the creative expression. The creative process is about trust; trusting yourself, the materials, and the mystery--all the while believing that the work will live and give life to you and the viewer.

Do you always have to share the meaning of the piece with the person we create it for?

No, I don't believe so. In fact, it can often rob the viewer of a special experience and their own unique interpretation of what the work is saying. However, if someone asks what you were thinking when you created it, then by all means, share. It might be more fun to tell them you would be happy to share, but first you'd love to hear what they are hearing it speak to them.

In my own journey, most of what God has used to speak life and light to others has usually been in spite of my creative intention going into a piece. Because of that, I always encourage artists to let the work you create speak. Let the process speak. Don't come into a piece of art thinking "this is what this is about" or "this is what I'm going to say". That will rob you of the process's beauty and impede the viewer's experience.

The beauty of art – the supernatural essence of what and how we create – is much more than what we bring to the studio. We bring ourselves and mix it with what Holy Spirit wants to do in and through us, and BOOM, what we create goes WAY beyond whatever we had in mind or could ever have done on our own. If we come into the process with a preconceived idea, we can miss the mystery of the Spirit's journey through us; the exponential result of our creative expression.

Are there certain colors, symbols and metaphors that must be used for art to be considered prophetic?

No. Many artists choose to incorporate Biblical symbology and metaphor into their work in typical and atypical ways, but there are no rules. The most powerful art is art that makes you wonder, think, consider and meditate on a deeper truth. If you use Biblical symbology or metaphor, do it in ways that are interesting, out of the box and atypical. Push the boundaries of what's "expected" and let the Holy Spirit lead you beyond your initial assumptions.

Do I have to be at a certain skill level artistically for God to use me?

Absolutely not! God can use you and your art at any place in your journey, guaranteed. However, growth in the Kingdom - and expanded influence, opportunity, resources and provision - is determined by how you steward your gifting.

No matter how gifted or talented an artist is, it's all for naught unless they nurture their connection with the Father. Being filled with the Spirit of God should always draw an artist into skill development so they can enlarge their capacity to be a conduit for God's Glory. Likewise, being filled and skilled should also lead artists who are growing in maturity to see their lives spilled out in the service of others. Teach what you know. Give outrageously. Teach your secrets. Be a river of giving, not a stagnant, fearful puddle who is satisfied to live off of yesterday's revelation.

For Further Reading

The following resources have been valuable to me in my understanding of prophetic art, the Kingdom and creating with the Holy Spirit.

- *Biblical Foundations for Prophetic Art* by Jörn Lange
- *Scribbling in the Sand* by Michael Card
- *Breath for the Bones* by Luci Shaw
- *Art + Faith* by Makoto Fujimura
- *Finding Divine Inspiration* by J. Scott McElroy
- *The Sound of Life's Unspeakable Beauty* by Martin Schleske
- *The Artist's Way* by Julia Cameron
- *Art for God's Sake* by Phillip Graham Ryken,
- *Power of Imagination* by Andrew Wommack
- *Imagination Redeemed* by Gene Edward Veith Jr.
- *Fixing Your Faith* by Gary Keesee
- *Spirit Born Creativity* by Mark & Patti Virkler,
- *Creativity in the Bible Parts 1 & 2* by Dr. Barry Liesch
- *Surprised by Hope* by NT Wright

About the Author

Matt is a woven sculpture artist from Asheville, North Carolina, and an internationally known Christian speaker, author of several books. He is also a mentor to artists from around the world through his "Created to Thrive" Artist Mentoring Program and The Thriving Christian Artist podcast.

In 2009, God called Matt to "raise up an army of artists to reveal His glory all over the earth." Since then, Matt has given his life to helping artists thrive spiritually, creatively, and in business through creating live events, resources, and online opportunities that equip artists to live the life they were divinely designed to live in the Kingdom.

As an artist, Matt's work has been featured in many magazines, shows, and exhibitions and is mostly commissioned by private clients for luxury mountain and coastal homes around the country. In 2011, Matt was recognized by the Smithsonian American Art Museum's Renwick Gallery as an American Artist Under 40. In 2018, Matt was recognized as one of the Best Artist Mentors in the country by Professional Artist Magazine.

Other Resources from Matt Tommey

Books by Matt Tommey
To see Matt's full line of books, visit
MattTommeyMentoring.com/resources

The Thriving Christian Artist Podcast
Matt's podcast can be found at
MattTommeyMentoring.com/podcast

Matt's Blog
If you love the podcast, then check out
Matt's weekly blog that picks up
where the podcast ends found at
MattTommeyMentoring.com/blog

The Artist Mentoring Program
An easy to follow online program
dedicated to helping Christian artists
become confident and equipped in their
creative callings. Learn More, visit
MattTommeyMentoring.com/artmentor

Made in the USA
Middletown, DE
21 March 2023

27343374R00066